The Old Recipe Book

Written by Ben Smith
Illustrated by Joy Antonie

"No one ever opens me up and makes my recipes," said the Old Recipe Book on the top shelf. "How come you younger books always get taken down and looked at? Why do you think Uncle Jack always makes food from the recipes on your pages?"

"Well Uncle Jack likes sweet things," said Cakes and Cookies, "that's why he uses me a lot. He just has to have sweet things."

"Uncle Jack likes to make lots of things for lunch," said Soups and Starters. "That's why Uncle Jack uses me a lot."

"Uncle Jack needs to get slim," said Summer Salads. "That's why he uses me a lot. He needs to eat salads."

"Uncle Jack likes to have his friends over," said Mexican Magic and Interesting Italian. "We have the best food for Uncle Jack's friends."

"Perhaps it's just because you're plain," said Fabulous French. "Look at us. We're all bright and glossy with lots of pictures. You're just plain and dull and old. And no pictures at all. We don't even know what sort of recipes you have inside your pages."

"Perhaps that's it," sighed the Old Recipe Book. "Perhaps it's because I'm just plain and dull and old. I wonder why Uncle Jack doesn't just throw me away?"

"Perhaps he will next time he's sorting things out," said Delicious Desserts. "I heard Uncle Jack telling a friend he was going to sort out some of his old things soon."

"What sort of recipes have you got in you anyway?" asked Soups and Starters.

"I've got all sorts," replied the Old Recipe Book. "I've got soups and starters and salads and main courses and desserts."

"Perhaps that's why Uncle Jack doesn't use you," said Summer Salads. "You have too many things in you."

"We don't think that will be why," said Fabulous French, Mexican Magic, and Interesting Italian. "He uses us and we've got recipes for soups and starters and salads and main courses and desserts too."

"It must be because you're plain then," said Fabulous French.

Just then Uncle Jack came into the kitchen with a woman the recipe books had never seen before. She looked up at the shelf.

"What lovely recipe books," she said. "Do you like to cook?"

"Yes, I love to cook," replied Uncle Jack. "One day I'll cook for you."

The woman came over and looked at the names on the recipe books.

"You have so many different books. Which one do you like the best?" she asked.

Uncle Jack reached up to the shelf and took down the plain, old, dull recipe book. He opened it up gently.

"This is the book I like best of all," he told her. "This was my mother's recipe book. It has all the recipes she made for our family when I was a little boy. I don't use it much now but it brings back lots and lots of happy memories. I will keep it forever."

"What a lucky man you are to have your mother's recipe book," the woman said.

Uncle Jack gently closed the Old Recipe Book and put it back on the shelf.

When Uncle Jack and his friend had gone, the Old Recipe Book looked at the other books and said, "I may be old and dull and plain but I'm the one he likes the best of all."